ECOSYSTEMS
IN ACTION

# LIFE IN A WETLAND

# LIFE IN A WETLAND

MELISSA STEWART

PHOTOGRAPHS BY STEPHEN K. MAKA

Lerner Publications Company
Minneapolis

**For Doug**

Lerner Publications Company
A division of Lerner Publishing Group
241 First Avenue North
Minneapolis, Minnesota 55401 U.S.A.

Website address: www.lernerbooks.com

Library of Congress Cataloging-in-Publication Data

Stewart, Melissa.
    Life in a wetland / by Melissa Stewart.
        p.    cm. — (Ecosystems in action)
    Summary: Describes the ecology of plants and animals in Everglades National Park, a wetland in south Florida.
        ISBN: 0–8225–4687–6 (lib. bdg. : alk. paper)
        1. Wetland ecology—Florida—Everglades National Park—Juvenile literature.
    [1. Wetland ecology. 2. Ecology. 3. Everglades National Park (Fla.)]  I. Title.
    II. Series.
    QH105.F6 S754  2003
    577.68—dc21                                                     2002011833

Manufactured in the United States of America
1 2 3 4 5 6 – JR – 08 07 06 05 04 03

# CONTENTS

INTRODUCTION
**WHAT IS AN ECOSYSTEM?**                                                6

CHAPTER 1
**THE EVERGLADES REGION: A NATURAL HISTORY**                             9

CHAPTER 2
**THE TRUE EVERGLADES**                                                  16

CHAPTER 3
**THE HIGHER GROUND**                                                    28

CHAPTER 4
**A LANDSCAPE SHAPED BY SALT**                                           38

CHAPTER 5
**MAINTAINING THE BALANCE**                                             49

CHAPTER 6
**HOW PEOPLE AFFECT THE EVERGLADES ECOSYSTEM**                          57

**WHAT YOU CAN DO**                                                      66

**WEBSITES AND FURTHER READING**                                         68

**GLOSSARY**                                                             69

**INDEX**                                                                71

# WHAT IS AN ECOSYSTEM?

If you look at any map of Florida, one of the first things you'll notice is a large green area at the state's southern tip. This is Everglades National Park. Most national parks preserve geological or scenic features, but Everglades National Park protects an ecosystem—a community of plants, animals, and other living organisms and their physical environment. The physical or nonliving elements in an ecosystem include the climate, the soil, the water, and the air.

Even though Everglades National Park covers 1.5 million acres (0.6 million hectares), it represents less than 20 percent of the entire Everglades ecosystem. The Everglades region is a giant wetland that covers nearly all the land south of Orlando.

In a wetland, the water table lies at or near the surface of the ground for most of the year. Some areas in the Everglades region are covered with swamps. These wetlands are flooded for at least part of the year and can support trees such as cypresses and mangroves. The region's vast, sawgrass-covered flatlands are more accurately described as marshes. Marshes are flooded for most or all of the year, and only grassy plants can grow there. Sloughs, a third kind of wetland, have formed in the Everglades region's lowest-lying areas. A slough contains more water than either a marsh or a swamp and is carpeted with a deep layer of squishy mud.

Many different kinds of wetlands are found all over the world. Prairie potholes form on grasslands in the midwestern United States. Dense, spongy bogs cover large areas of land in Canada and northern Europe. Estuaries are wetlands in places where freshwater from a river mixes with salty ocean water. Because all these watery environments have many things in common, wetlands are grouped together as one of Earth's biomes.

A biome is an extensive natural community of living organisms. Forests,

oceans, deserts, and grasslands are all biomes. The Sonoran Desert in the southwestern United States is one ecosystem in the desert biome, while the East African savanna is an ecosystem in the grasslands biome. All the ecosystems in a biome have much more in common with one another than with ecosystems in other biomes. For that reason, scientists are more likely to compare the Everglades region with Okefenokee Swamp in Georgia or a bog in Ireland than with a tropical rain forest in Costa Rica or the hot, dry Australian outback.

As in every other ecosystem on Earth, the organisms that live in the Everglades region need energy to grow and reproduce. The ultimate source of this energy is the sun. In most ecosystems, green plants are the key primary producers. They make their own food by absorbing energy from sunlight and changing it into chemical energy through photosynthesis.

Primary consumers are animals that eat primary producers. When a primary consumer, such as an apple snail, grazes on primary producers, such as algae, the stored energy in the algae passes into the snail's body. In turn, secondary consumers obtain the energy they need to live and grow by preying on primary consumers.

When organisms die, they provide food for decomposers. As decomposers break down dead plants and animals, they release nutrients into the soil. Sawgrass and other Everglades plants absorb the nutrients from the soil and use them to carry out important functions. In this way, energy and nutrients continuously cycle through the ecosystem.

> **AS IN EVERY OTHER ECOSYSTEM ON EARTH, THE ORGANISMS THAT LIVE IN THE EVERGLADES REGION NEED ENERGY TO GROW AND REPRODUCE. THE ULTIMATE SOURCE OF THIS ENERGY IS THE SUN.**

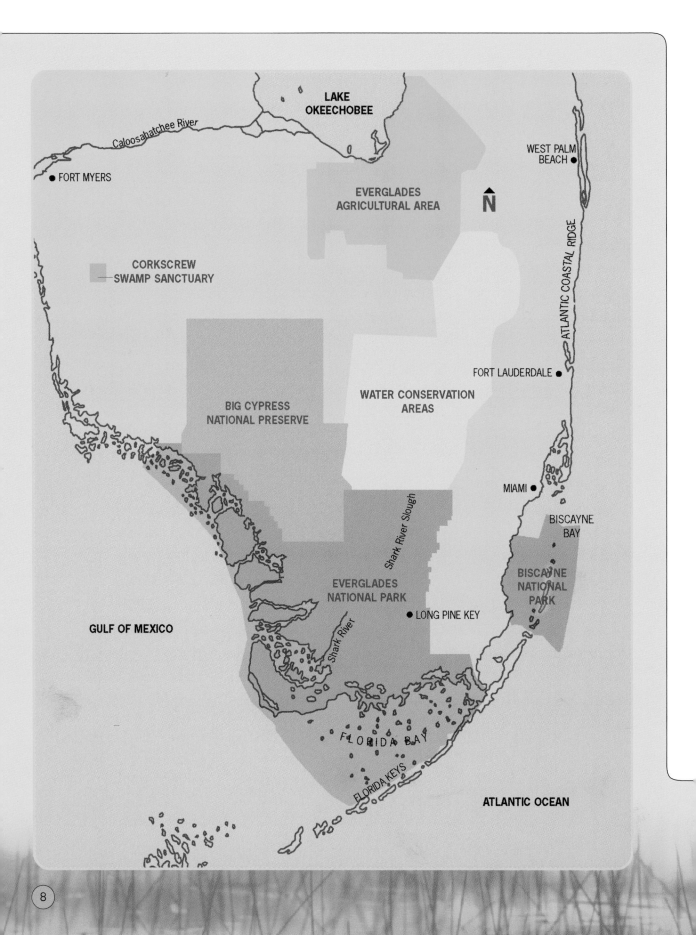

LAKE OKEECHOBEE

Caloosahatchee River

• FORT MYERS

EVERGLADES AGRICULTURAL AREA

WEST PALM BEACH •

N

CORKSCREW SWAMP SANCTUARY

ATLANTIC COASTAL RIDGE

FORT LAUDERDALE •

WATER CONSERVATION AREAS

BIG CYPRESS NATIONAL PRESERVE

MIAMI •

BISCAYNE BAY

Shark River Slough

EVERGLADES NATIONAL PARK

BISCAYNE NATIONAL PARK

GULF OF MEXICO

Shark River

• LONG PINE KEY

FLORIDA BAY

FLORIDA KEYS

ATLANTIC OCEAN

# CHAPTER 1

# THE EVERGLADES REGION: A NATURAL HISTORY

The Everglades region stretches across the southern third of the Florida peninsula. It is bordered by the Atlantic Ocean on the east and the Gulf of Mexico on the west. The southernmost areas of the Everglades merge with the salty waters of Florida Bay. The region's northern border is more difficult to define, but most people agree that it includes Lake Okeechobee—one of the Everglades ecosystem's most important features.

Millions of years ago, the Everglades region was covered by a shallow sea. Ancient rivers flowing into this sea brought huge loads of sandy sediment. When the fast-flowing freshwater of the rivers mixed with the slower-moving seawater, the sediment drifted to the bottom. As microscopic sea creatures died, their tiny skeletons and shells also fell to the seafloor.

The action of waves sorted the sediment, skeletons, and shells into a series of horizontal layers, with the larger particles on the bottom and the smaller

**LAKE OKEECHOBEE**

bits at the top. Over thousands of years, the weight of the upper layers pressed down on the lower layers. All that pressure squeezed out the water and cemented the materials together to form layer upon layer of limestone rock. The surface of this thick limestone bed was smooth and flat, with a gentle downward tilt to the southwest. This rock, which still underlies large areas of the Everglades region, played a critical role in creating one of the world's most special ecosystems.

## HIGH GROUND HISTORY

Other parts of the Everglades region formed during the Ice Age. Between 1.7 million and 12,000 years ago, temperature shifts affecting the entire planet caused glaciers to spread out over large areas of land and then retreat at least four times. Although the glaciers never reached as far as South Florida, the area was still affected by the cycles of freezing and thawing.

Each time the glaciers grew, much of the world's water supply became locked up in ice sheets. In some areas, sea level fell by as much as 300 feet (90 meters). Large areas of seafloor were exposed to the air, and untold numbers of marine animals died. Strong winds eroded, or wore away, some areas and transported the material to new places. This formed the slightly elevated terrain underneath Big Cypress Swamp, northwest of Everglades National Park.

During the times between glaciers, ice melted and sea level rose. Strong ocean currents picked up and carried the shells and skeletons of the dead creatures. But as the currents shifted and changed direction, they lost speed

**ALTHOUGH THE GLACIERS NEVER REACHED AS FAR AS SOUTH FLORIDA, THE AREA WAS STILL AFFECTED BY THE CYCLES OF FREEZING AND THAWING.**

and dumped the material. As huge piles of shells and skeletons accumulated and were packed together, they formed the Atlantic Coastal Ridge, which lies under a narrow strip of elevated land along Florida's east coast.

## WATER COMES AND GOES

Each time the Ice Age glaciers advanced, they scraped the earth, eroding mountains and carving out craters. Later, when the glaciers receded, thousands of new lakes were created as meltwater became trapped in the craters.

Most of the earth's major lakes are sprinkled across the Northern Hemisphere. These Ice Age relics hold water that once filled the seas and oceans. By the time the last glaciers had retreated to the north, sea level was significantly lower throughout the world. The sea that had once covered South Florida no longer existed. It was replaced by a vast wetland that waxed and waned with the seasons.

Unlike most of North America, South Florida does not experience four distinct seasons. Because the area is close to the equator, it remains fairly warm all year

SOUTHERN FLORIDA HAS BEEN COVERED BY AN ENORMOUS WETLAND
SINCE THE END OF THE MOST RECENT ICE AGE.

long. As a result, there are really just two seasons. Summers are hot and wet, while winters are warm and dry. From May to November, the blue skies and cottony clouds of midmorning are replaced with towering thunderheads each afternoon. They deliver as much as 65 inches (170 centimeters) of rain to the region during the wet season. During the dry season, from December to April, rainfall is rare.

As soon as the rains stop, surface water begins to disappear. Some is absorbed by the porous limestone rock, but most of it evaporates. By March most of the Everglades region is parched. The drought continues until another season of rain renews the land.

## THE EVOLUTION OF AN ECOSYSTEM

The Everglades ecosystem began to emerge about five thousand years ago. At first only a few hardy plants could tolerate the annual cycles of flood and drought on the exposed limestone plain. During each wet season, these stalwart survivors flowered and produced seeds. During the dry season, the plants withered and died. But the seeds they left behind sprouted during the next wet season and grew into a new generation of greenery.

As the remains of these first plants accumulated and decayed over time, a layer of rich, spongy soil developed on top of the limestone. But all the soil was not created equal. The kind of soil that formed in a particular area depended on the kind of plants that lived there. And the kind of plants that grew in an area depended on the land's hydroperiod—the amount of time the ground was underwater each year. Hydroperiod, in turn, was determined by elevation, or height above sea level.

Compared to most places, the Everglades region is flat. It has no tall mountains or deep valleys, no gently rolling hills and dales. The entire area lies less than 20 feet (6 meters) above sea level, with elevations generally averaging between 7 and 10 feet (2 to 3 meters). In a New England forest or an Arizona desert, such subtle differences have no noticeable impact on the landscape. But in South Florida, little differences mean a lot.

In the Everglades region, small changes in elevation determine whether an area will be a flooded, muddy slough or a vast, open marshland of gently swaying sawgrass. In lowland sloughs, the spongy, light brown soil is ideal for growing water lilies, spatterdock, bladderwort, and other floating plants. The dark, rich soil underlying sawgrass marshes is better suited for tall, grassy plants, such as sedges and reeds.

Move just a bit higher and you enter another world. The sawgrass community is abruptly replaced by the thick, tangled vegetation of a hardwood hammock (a small island) or a cool, dark cypress swamp. In these environments, water is always close to the surface, but the land is flooded for only a few months each year. The soil in the more elevated areas drains more quickly than in marshes or sloughs because it contains some sand. Move upward just a bit more, and the lush landscape gives way to sandy pinelands. Since these pine forests are dry for most of the year, wildfires periodically flare up, reshaping the landscape.

(TOP) **SAWGRASS *(CLADIUM JAMAICENSE)***

(BOTTOM) **A BALD CYPRESS *(TAXODIUM DISTICHUM)* SWAMP**

13

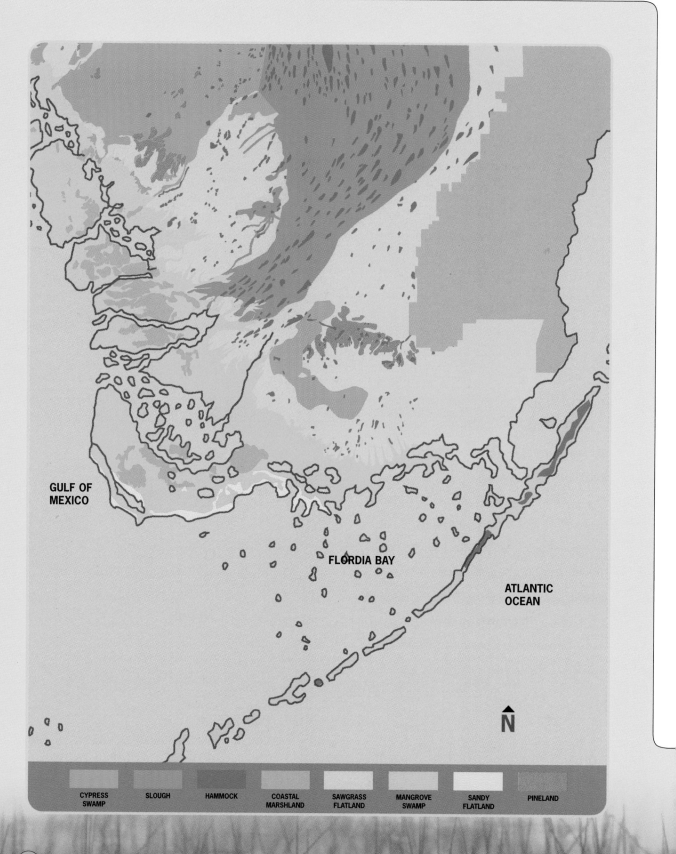

GULF OF
MEXICO

FLORDIA BAY

ATLANTIC
OCEAN

Ñ

CYPRESS SWAMP    SLOUGH    HAMMOCK    COASTAL MARSHLAND    SAWGRASS FLATLAND    MANGROVE SWAMP    SANDY FLATLAND    PINELAND

In the southernmost reaches of the Everglades ecosystem, salt plays a more important role than elevation and soil in determining the look of the land. As freshwater from the northern and central Everglades region flows toward Florida Bay, the water mixes with salty seawater that surges onto the land twice each day at high tide. Most plants cannot survive in this salty environment, but mangroves can. As a result, these short, dense trees dominate the southern Everglades region.

Scattered among the twisted clusters of mangroves, sandy flatlands mark the spots where hurricanes have unleashed their fury on the Florida peninsula. Where mangroves have been destroyed, dense mats of pickerelweed, glasswort, and saltwort cover the land.

Once plant communities were firmly established in the Everglades region, large numbers of animals began to arrive. Many species of mammals, reptiles, and amphibians migrated to the area from the north. Birds came from the north and from the Caribbean Islands to the east. Fish and other aquatic creatures were swept into the area from northern rivers and southern seas. Each animal species moved through the region until it found the environmental conditions and plant community that it needed to survive. Some animals settled in the lowland sloughs, while others searched for drier spots, such as pinelands.

For thousands of years, the land and the life-forms in the Everglades region developed and changed together. While many species have come and gone, the survivors remain because they could cope with frequent shifts in the ecosystem's conditions. Over time, these hardy organisms developed features and behaviors that help them endure floods and droughts, wildfires and hurricanes. The combination of an ever-changing physical environment and a diverse collection of inhabitants is what makes the Everglades region an important and unique ecosystem.

# CHAPTER 2

# THE TRUE EVERGLADES

The Everglades region occupies most of South Florida, but its heart and soul is the unique "everlasting glades" of sawgrass for which the area was named. Originally, these prairielike marshlands began just south of Lake Okeechobee and swept southward all the way to Florida Bay. Even though most of the sawgrass-covered marshland is long gone, it is still possible to imagine how water flowed naturally through the area for close to five thousand years.

Throughout the year, the meandering Kissimmee River delivered water and sediment to Lake Okeechobee, the second largest lake entirely within the borders of the United States. With a maximum depth of only 17 feet (5.2 meters), the shallow lake couldn't possibly hold all the water that arrived during the wet season. Huge quantities of water spilled over the banks at the southern end of Lake Okeechobee. As the broad sheet of water slowly spread across the land, it replenished sloughs and flooded the thirsty sawgrass.

Everglades sloughs often contained as much as 3 feet (1 meter) of water, but the blanket of water covering the surrounding sawgrass flatlands was usually no more than

**SAWGRASS (CLADIUM JAMAICENSE) COVERS THE "TRUE EVERGLADES."**

6 inches (15 centimeters) deep. Creeping slowly southward, the shallow "river of grass" journeyed more than 100 miles (160 kilometers) before emptying into Florida Bay.

At the height of the wet season, Everglades water covered an area of land about 50 miles (80 kilometers) wide. On the east, the "river of grass" was bordered by a pineland growing on the Atlantic Coastal Ridge. On the west, the water was contained by slightly higher land dominated by cypress trees. The true Everglades—the strip of land between the pineland ridge and the cypress swamp—was shaped like a long spoon tilted slightly to the southwest. The Lake Okeechobee shoreline formed the bowl end of the spoon (where the handle would attach), while the tip of the spoon's handle discharged water into Florida Bay.

> THE TRUE EVERGLADES—THE STRIP OF LAND BETWEEN THE PINELAND RIDGE AND THE CYPRESS SWAMP—WAS SHAPED LIKE A LONG SPOON TILTED SLIGHTLY TO THE SOUTHWEST.

## THE LOWEST LAND

Sawgrass marshlands dominate the true Everglades landscape, but the lowest land cannot support this plant. In sloughs the hydroperiod is nearly 11 months long and water is often more than 12 inches (30 centimeters) deep. A variety of aquatic plants gently bob in the faster-flowing water of these muddy areas.

The largest Everglades slough is the Shark River Slough, in the northeast corner of Everglades National Park. When water is plentiful, water lilies, floating hearts, spatterdock, and maidencane spread across the water's surface. These large-leaved aquatic plants contain vast supplies of chlorophyll, the primary plant pigment that absorbs sunlight and makes photosynthesis possible.

A slough plant called bladderwort occasionally supplements its diet with a bit of animal meat. When a water insect brushes against one of the plant's tiny flattened sacs, the insect is sucked in as the sac expands. Over the next few days, the bladderwort's digestive juices slowly break down the insect's body.

Below the water's surface are spongy mats of periphyton. Periphyton is a community of several dozen species of microorganisms that live on a mineral called calcite. These tiny creatures form the base of the true Everglades' food chain. Periphyton is the major source of nourishment for snails, crayfish, and other invertebrates, or animals without backbones. (Animals with backbones are called vertebrates. They include mammals, fish, reptiles, amphibians, and birds.) Wood ducks and red-bellied turtles also dine on periphyton, as do feeder fishes such as sailfin mollies, flagfish, and sheepshead minnows. These small fishes are among the preferred prey for larger fishes, snapping turtles, and some wading birds.

As these hunters catch fish below the water's surface, a female purple gallinule scampers across a carpet of lily pads in search of tasty seeds, snails, and insects. When the brightly colored, chicken-sized bird has had her fill, she plucks a leaf from a nearby plant. She clumsily flits back to her woven reed nest and offers the leaf to her mate. The male adds the leaf to the nest and then hops to the ground. While he takes a turn feeding, the female takes over incubation duty, keeping their clutch of eight eggs warm and safe.

High above the gallinules, clouds drift across a bright blue morning sky. Suddenly the land darkens as a great blue heron momentarily blocks out the sun's rays. The huge, lanky bird glides gracefully through the air, slowly flapping its massive wings and dragging its long, sticklike legs behind. After passing over the slough, the heron abruptly swings around and begins to descend. It has discovered a good place to fish.

The heron slowly wades through the slough's shallow water. When it spots a potential meal, the bird extends its folded neck and stabs the unsuspecting fish with

its long, spearlike bill. The bird quickly devours its catch. Then it shakes out its wings and transforms its body into a lean, straight pole. As the bird suns itself among the sawgrass and reeds alongside the slough, it is nearly invisible to its enemies.

If a hungry alligator happens to be lurking nearby, its attention is much more likely to be drawn to a different wading bird, a glossy black anhinga perched on a rock with its waterlogged wings spread wide. After a morning of diving for fish, the anhinga is taking a break. Most wading birds have a special gland that releases oil to make their feathers water-resistant, but the anhinga does not. It must dry its soaked wings in the hot sun.

In another part of the slough, a group of frolicking freshwater otters chirp and whistle as they dive and roll, wrestle, and play a game of water tag. Their sleek bodies, webbed hind feet, and short, muscular legs make them strong, graceful swimmers. After an afternoon of fun, the otters rest briefly and then begin to hunt at dusk.

Otters usually dine on fish and crayfish, but they are not picky eaters.

(ABOVE) **PURPLE GALLINULE**
*(PORPHYRULA MARTINICA)*

(RIGHT) **GREAT BLUE HERON**
*(ARDEA HERODIAS)*

They are perfectly willing to eat snakes and snails, tadpoles and turtles, dragonflies and ducklings. They may even devour baby alligators. To find crayfish and other bottom dwellers, an otter dives down and pokes its stiff, bristly whiskers into cracks and crevices between rocks. When the otter's supersensitive whiskers detect prey, the animal digs furiously until it can grab its dinner.

## A SEA OF SAWGRASS

While otters hunt for their evening meal in the slough, raccoons awaken and begin exploring the sawgrass flatlands that flank the muddy water. Like otters, raccoons prefer fish and crayfish but will eat almost anything. Using their nimble, handlike paws, these furry masked hunters spend their nights probing the watery wilderness for snails and shellfish or stealing the eggs of reptiles and birds. One raccoon finds a freshwater clam, cracks open the shell with its tough teeth, and slurps out the soft animal inside. It is the height of the wet season, so food is plentiful, and all the raccoons eat well. As the sun rises, they scamper back to their dens with their bellies full.

While raccoons sleep the day away, many other creatures go about the business of living. A doe and her white-spotted fawn wade through the sawgrass in search of the plants' hardy, reddish-brown flowers. The deer also munch on the spike rush, water hyssop, and marsh mermaid plants growing among the sawgrass.

**RIVER OTTER (*LUTRA CANADENSIS*)**

# SAWGRASS ISN'T GRASS *(Cladium jamaicense)*

Large areas of the Everglades region are covered with gently swaying sawgrass. This hardy plant can survive flooding and fire and requires only low levels of nutrients. While the sawgrass in many areas stands about 3 feet (1 meter) tall, in some places it rises more than 10 feet (3 meters) above the water's surface. Sawgrass grows tallest in spots with thick soil. It is most dense in places with a long hydroperiod.

Despite its name, sawgrass is not really a kind of grass. Grasses have round, hollow stems, but sawgrass has a solid, triangular stem. This makes it a member of the sedge family. The long, stiff blades of sawgrass are lined with upward-pointing teeth that slice the skin of people who try to walk through it. Besides protecting the plant from hungry herbivores (plant-eating animals), the teeth help collect dew during dry spells. While few creatures eat the barbed blades of sawgrass, some do feed on its small flowers and tiny brown seeds.

The seeds of many plants are dispersed by the wind or in the droppings of fruit-eating animals, but sawgrass seeds simply drop into the water. The seeds lie dormant throughout the dry season and sprout when the rains return. Sometimes sawgrass seeds fail to germinate, but that's not a major problem because the plant has another way of reproducing. Sawgrass is a plant with rhizomes—fleshy stems that grow horizontally underground. Rhizomes are most often used to store food, but they may also develop roots and shoots and grow into new plants.

(TOP) **GRASS FROG** *(PSEUDACRIS OCULARIS)*

(BOTTOM) **APPLE SNAIL** *(POMACEA)*

As the deer feed, they are serenaded by the gentle chorus of oak toads and the harsh oinking call of pig frogs. But the smallest Everglades frog remains silent. The grass frog spends its days clinging to sawgrass, but sings for a mate only at night. When it spies a hungry snowy egret overhead, the tiny grass frog drops into the water and swims to safety.

The frog's narrow escape does not discourage the egret. A moment later, it sets its sights on three crayfish lodged in the dense sawgrass. The egret quickly grabs the invertebrates, swallows them whole, and flies off in search of more prey. In its haste, the bird doesn't even notice a cluster of pearly white eggs clinging to a nearby blade of sawgrass.

In a few weeks, the eggs will hatch and two dozen tiny apple snails will crawl down the plant into the water. Almost immediately, the young snails will begin grazing on the green algae that coat the rocks just below the water's surface.

Green algae are members of a large, diverse group of simple organisms called protists. Green algae form large, complex colonies of cells that live and work together.

The colonies, which grow and spread along the surfaces of submerged rocks and logs, resemble slimy, miniature forests. Green algae are primary producers. The energy they capture through photosynthesis is transferred up the food chain to primary consumers such as apple snails.

Apple snails spend most of their day feeding, but they are often interrupted. Every few minutes, they must glide up a blade of spiky sawgrass to the water's surface to get a breath of air. Unlike a fish, apple snails do not have gills, and therefore cannot remove oxygen from the water.

Snails are small and slow, so they are attractive to many Everglades predators. The energy and nutrients stored in the snails' bodies provide hungry hunters—the secondary consumers—with the raw materials their own bodies need for breathing, blood circulation, brain activity, muscle movements, and other life-sustaining processes. Wading birds, raccoons, otters, and young alligators are just a few of the animals that enjoy an occasional meal of snails. But there is one Everglades hunter that feeds almost exclusively on apple snails.

On a warm summer afternoon, a male snail kite circles high above the sawgrass in search of a meal. As soon as the keen-sighted bird spots an apple snail, he drops down to the water's surface. Using his sharp talons, the kite plucks the prey out of the water. Then the bird lands nearby to investigate his catch. The kite's long, hooked beak is perfectly shaped for prying the soft-bodied snail out of its protective shell.

Like his relatives the hawks and eagles, the snail kite is a skilled flier and hunter. When water is plentiful, the snail kite spends most of his time feeding. A few months after the rains stop, he begins to look for a mate. When he spots a female, the kite loops and dives through the air to get her attention. Then he brings her food or nesting materials. When the female is satisfied by his showmanship, the birds mate and then search for a good place to build a nest.

## WHEN SOIL BUILDS UP, TREES APPEAR

It doesn't take the kites very long to find the perfect nesting spot—a low shrub growing along the watery edge of a tree island, or hammock. Like an island in a lake, a hammock is a small area of land that rises above the surrounding landscape. Hundreds of hammocks are scattered throughout Everglades sloughs and sawgrass flatlands.

Although most hardwood hammocks occupy fewer than 10 acres (4 hectares) of land, they are an important part of the Everglades ecosystem. Because hammocks do not flood annually, they can support more than two dozen species of tropical and temperate trees and shrubs. Two or three times as many species of plants and animals live on hammocks as in the surrounding marshland. The dense vegetation provides excellent nesting sites for a variety of Everglades birds, including snail kites.

When the kites have finished building their messy stick nest, the female lays three eggs. For the next month, the birds take turns incubating the eggs. When the chicks hatch, the parents begin to search furiously for food. It takes a lot of apple snails for a kite chick to grow big and strong. After about one month, the young kites are ready for their first flight. They

stand on top of the nest, spread their wings wide, and flap with all their might until they rise into the sky. Now they will be able to hunt for themselves. In just a few more weeks, the young kites will leave the nest for good.

Many other animals spend most or all of their lives on Everglades hammocks. The intertwined shrubs and vines growing along the edges of a hammock provide a perfect place for a gray fox to make its den and sleep the day away. At night the fox hunts for birds, invertebrates, fruits and berries, small mammals and reptiles, fish, and eggs. If the fox is suddenly frightened by an unfamiliar noise or a predator, it scurries up the nearest tree and waits for the danger to pass.

Inside the tree island's tangled border, the landscape suddenly changes. There are fewer shrubs and more tall trees. A red-shouldered hawk perches in a tall, straight live oak tree and scans the surrounding sawgrass for snakes and small rodents. Cardinals and blue jays build nests in red maples, while a yellow-crowned night heron roosts in a nearby willow. Sprinkled

among the temperate forest trees are some less familiar tropical species, including paradise trees, lysilomas, cocoplums, wild coffees, cabbage palms, inkwoods, and poisonwoods. Poisonwoods can cause an itchy skin rash.

Just below the leafy canopy formed by tree branches, an assortment of air plants thrive in the moisture-laden air of midsummer. Unlike most plants, the roots of air plants do not grow in the ground. The sweet scent of butterfly orchids fills the air, while the spiky, fuchsia brackets of bromeliads punctuate the landscape with color. During the dry season, resurrection ferns curl up, but when the rain returns, these plants quickly spring back to life.

At one end of the hammock, the roots of a strangler fig wrap themselves around the smooth red bark of a gumbo-limbo tree. The roots prevent the helpless host tree from growing outward. As the fig grows, its leafy canopy expands and blocks out sunlight that the gumbo-limbo needs to carry out photosynthesis. Eventually, the host will die and decompose. By then the fig's thick roots will be strong enough for the plant to stand on its own.

In another part of the hammock, a mother raccoon raises a litter of kits inside a rotting West Indian mahogany tree. The youngsters don't seem to mind the persistent jackhammering of a pileated woodpecker pecking at the tree in search of grubs. Over time, the busy activity of woodpeckers, bacteria, and fungi will weaken the tree, and it will topple over. Then it will make a good home for an eastern coral snake, a scarlet snake, or a scarlet king snake. These three reptiles

**EVERGLADES HAMMOCKS**

look similar—black with brightly colored rings that warn predators to stay away. But only the eastern coral snake is poisonous.

An eastern coral snake may also choose to hide in a rocky crevice. When the snake gets hungry, it slithers out and weaves among the leaf litter in search of smaller snakes and lizards. It ignores the army of young eastern lubber grasshoppers marching across the ground. The recently hatched nymphs are searching for a tree with tasty leaves.

As the nymphs grow, they molt, or shed their hard outer covering, five times.

When they emerge from their final molt, they are yellowish brown with black markings and have stubby wings that cannot be used for flying. Sharp spikes on their hind legs contain a foul-smelling chemical that will sicken most enemies.

But when a new adult grasshopper stumbles into the web of a female golden orb weaver spider, the predator is ready for action. She sprints across her trap to investigate. She works quickly to wrap layer after layer of silky thread around the grasshopper's wriggling body. Finally, she plunges her venom-filled fangs into the

(ABOVE) **EASTERN LUBBER GRASSHOPPER *(ROMALEA GUTTATA)***

(OPPOSITE PAGE) **GOLDEN ORB WEAVER SPIDER *(ARGIOPE AURANTIA)***

victim until it stops struggling. The grasshopper is dead.

In all the excitement, the web has been torn apart. The spider quickly sucks out the grasshopper's insides and then begins rebuilding her trap. She lifts her abdomen to release silky strands from her spinnerets. She weaves the sticky threads into a wheel-shaped web nearly 2 feet (0.6 meter) across. Oil coating the spider's body prevents her from becoming entangled in her web.

All the while, a tiny male golden orb weaver has been constructing a smaller, messier web at the outer edge of the female's. He has come to mate with her. When the female signals that she is ready, the male approaches. After the spiders mate, the female devours the male. Then she makes a brown, papery sac that contains between 300 and 1,400 eggs. She attaches it to one side of her web.

As dusk descends on the Everglades hammock, the spider settles down for a much-needed rest. Below her, a wood rat scurries across the forest floor in search of cover. It has just heard the hooting of a barred owl and knows that danger is near.

But the wood rat is lucky. The grayish brown, puffy-headed owl doesn't see the little rodent. The bird is too busy filling the air with its mellow cries. A moment later, it stops calling, stretches its wings wide, and gracefully ascends into the evening sky. Tonight the bird will travel a long distance in search of food.

# CHAPTER 3

# THE HIGHER GROUND

The owl flies silently over a slough and crosses a wide area of sawgrass. The marshland is usually a good place to hunt for water rats, but not tonight. The owl keeps flying and the landscape begins to change. The bird leaves behind the fields of sawgrass and enters Big Cypress Swamp. Located northwest of Everglades National Park, this huge area of swampland includes most of Big Cypress National Preserve, Corkscrew Swamp Sanctuary, and all the land in between.

## WHERE DWARF CYPRESSES RULE

The owl lands in the crown of a dwarf cypress tree near the edge of Big Cypress National Preserve. The sharp-sighted bird surveys the area below for prey—and predators. The land here is slightly higher than the sawgrass marshlands the owl has just flown over. The thin, sandy soil supports forests of dwarf cypress trees as well as ash, custard apple, red maple, willow, and oak trees. In low-lying areas where the limestone bed has crumbled away, the dwarf cypress trees grow in crowded clumps. The tallest trees are in the center and the shortest trees are on the outside. As a result, the leafy canopy is shaped like a dome.

Like pines and spruces, dwarf cypress trees are conifers, but they are not evergreens. At the beginning of

**THE THIN, SANDY SOIL SUPPORTS FORESTS OF DWARF CYPRESS TREES AS WELL AS ASH, CUSTARD APPLE, RED MAPLE, WILLOW, AND OAK TREES.**

each dry season, a cypress's needlelike leaves turn golden brown and drift down to the ground. When the rains return in the spring, the tree sprouts dozens of new, green leaves.

Some cypress trees, especially those growing near sloughs or ponds, reach heights of more than 100 feet (30 meters). Dwarf cypresses are much shorter. Their growth is stunted because they live in soil that is thin, dry for much of the year, and low in nutrients. Even trees that are hundreds of years old rarely grow more than 25 feet (8 meters) tall. The average dwarf cypress is only 10 feet (3 meters) tall.

All cypress trees have "knees"—unusual structures that grow up from their root systems and rise above water level. These strange-looking growths may help the trees obtain carbon dioxide and other gases from the air. The knees also come in handy as sunning spots for snakes. Orchids, bromeliads, and other air plants grow on the structures as well.

## A NEW DAY DAWNS

As day breaks in the cypress swamp, it's time for the owl to sleep. Just as the bird is

**DWARF CYPRESS (TAXODIUM)**

about to shut its eyes, a Florida panther passes below. The large, tan-colored cat is returning to its den after an unsuccessful night of hunting. The young female panther has recently left her mother and is still struggling to establish a home range. She spends her days sleeping and her nights hunting for deer, wild hogs, raccoons, and rabbits. In a year or two, she will be old enough to find a mate and raise a family of her own.

As the swamp's nocturnal inhabitants drift off to sleep, a female cottonmouth snake begins her daily routine. She slithers up a cypress tree and stretches out on one of its knees. The snake spends the morning warming her body in the sun.

By noon the cottonmouth has warmed up and is ready to hunt. She slides off the tree and zips across the ground. Like rattlesnakes, the cottonmouth is a pit viper. Pit vipers have deep pits between their eyes and nostrils. The snakes use the pits to detect heat energy given off by warm-blooded prey, such as small mammals. Pit vipers also have deadly fangs that release venom into their prey.

The 4-foot-long (1-meter-long) cottonmouth soon catches a large rat. When she finishes eating the prey, the snake searches for a dark rocky crevice. She slips inside and waits. A few hours later, a dozen tiny, squiggling snakes come out of her body. The young snakes do not look like their mother. The adult cottonmouth is darkly colored, but the little ones are pale brown with reddish brown bands.

## AT HOME AMONG BALD CYPRESSES

Farther to the west, most of the land in Corkscrew Swamp Sanctuary is wetter and the trees are taller. Alongside sloughs and shallow ponds, ancient bald cypress trees rise more than 100 feet (30 meters) into the sky. During the wet season, the sweet songs of black-throated green warblers, yellow-billed cuckoos, pine warblers, and painted buntings fill the air. But as the long, dry winter approaches, the peaceful scene begins to change.

Corkscrew Swamp Sanctuary is a 10,000-acre (4,000-hectare) area that is home to the Everglades region's largest rookery, or nesting area, for wood storks. Each November, as the land dries out, storks arrive in droves. Their squawking drowns out the songs of the swamp's summer residents.

As soon as a male wood stork lands in the rookery, he finds a quiet, secluded place to nest. He establishes a small territory around that spot and challenges any rival storks that enter the area. At first, he chases away females too. But if a female returns several times and approaches him with an open bill and spread wings, he will let her get close. She has given him the signal that she is ready to mate.

For the next few days, the large, bald-headed birds spend most of their time building a messy stick nest in the crown of a tall cypress tree. Then the female lays three eggs. A month later, the eggs hatch. It is the height of the dry season, and many Everglades creatures are struggling to stay alive. Fish, frogs, and other aquatic animals compete for space in ever-shrinking pools. The pools provide easy pickings for wood storks with hungry chicks to feed.

**FLORIDA PANTHER (PUMA CONCOLOR CORYI)**

While the female stork guards the nest, the male flies off in search of the nearest water hole. He gorges himself with food and then returns to the nest. His mate greets him by bobbing her head. Then both parents throw back their heads, open their bills wide, and hiss loudly as they lower their bills and swing their heads from side to side.

Meanwhile, the hungry chicks scream, lower their heads, and raise their wings. They are begging for food. The male moves to the center of the nest and regurgitates an assortment of aquatic creatures, which the chicks greedily devour. But their growing bodies are not satisfied. Moments later, they are squawking again.

Now it's their mother's turn to hunt. While she is gone, the male watches the youngsters. Two of the chicks are larger than the third. They tease and pick at the smaller one. At feeding time, the larger chicks shove the little one aside so they can eat its share of the food. Stressed and starving, the little chick grows weaker every day. Eventually, its larger

siblings push the helpless chick out of the nest. This may seem cruel, but it will increase the other chicks' chances of survival. With one less mouth for the parents to feed, the two stronger chicks will get more food.

On the ground below the rookery, an alligator is waiting for stork weaklings to be cast out of their nests. These little birds make quick, easy meals. As the alligator patrols the area, it is actually helping the stork colony. The ferocious hunter scares away raccoons and other tree-climbing predators that would otherwise steal the birds' eggs or eat their chicks.

Wood storks are not the only birds that spend their winters in Corkscrew Swamp Sanctuary. Great egrets, white ibis, and little blue herons are just some of the wading birds that build nesting colonies in the swamp. Like the storks, they are attracted by the tall trees and the fish-filled pools and ponds.

Wood storks, great egrets, and white ibis are all similar-looking white birds. The wood stork is the largest of the three. It stands more than 3 feet (1 meter) tall and

**LITTLE BLUE HERON (EGRETTA CAERULEA)**

has long black legs, a black stripe below its wings, and a dark head and neck. The great egret is a bit smaller than a wood stork. It also has long black legs, but its head and long, gracefully curved neck are pure white. The white ibis is smaller still. It has long orange-red legs, a bright red face, and an orange-red bill.

Great egrets often feed alongside white ibis. The two birds do not compete for food, though, because they have different ways of hunting. Ibis use their long bills to probe for prey, while egrets hunt by sight. As a result, egrets often catch creatures that ibis stir up. Ibis also benefit from this team feeding, because egrets are more likely to notice alligators or land predators before they have a chance to attack. The egrets' screams let ibis know that danger is near.

Another swamp-dwelling wading bird, the little blue heron, is shaped like the great egret but is only about 2 feet (0.6 meter) tall. As an adult, it has a dark head and neck and a slate blue body. As a youngster, however, its feathers are pure white. The only way to distinguish a young heron from its egret relatives is by looking at its bill. Most egrets have a yellow bill, but a little blue heron's bill is grayish blue.

When a local slough gets crowded, one little blue heron decides to hunt for small snakes and lizards along the water's edge. But a crouching bobcat is waiting nearby for the right moment to pounce. The sharp-sighted bird detects a movement, but it's too late. A flash of reddish brown fur springs forward and grabs the bird by the neck. As both animals plunge into the

water, the heron screams and a flurry of feathers bursts into the air. Startled by all the commotion, nearby birds call out warnings and lift off into the sky.

The bobcat crawls ashore with its catch, shakes itself dry, and disappears into the vegetation. Out of sight, the feline eats its meal. Most of the time, the bobcat is active at night, but sometimes it hunts during the day.

A bobcat is smaller than a Florida panther, but the two cats inhabit the same areas. An adult bobcat is about 3 feet (0.9 meter) long and weighs up to 25 pounds (11 kilograms). It has a stubby tail and a golden-tan coat with stripes and patches of dark fur. Its belly, chest, and muzzle are often white. The bobcat's mottled colors blend well with the surrounding vegetation.

Many bobcats in the Everglades region spend only some of their time hunting in cypress swamps. The rest of the time, they prowl in the drier pineland forests.

## PINELAND FORESTS

While most of Big Cypress Swamp is covered with cypress swamps, the area

BOBCATS *(LYNX RUFUS)* CAN LEAP UP TO 12 FEET (4 METERS) TO CATCH PREY.

also supports some hardwood hammocks and scattered pineland patches. The land in these areas is slightly higher and drier than the surrounding terrain.

Pine forests grow in the thinnest, sandiest soil and on the highest land in the Everglades region. Pinelands receive the same amount of rainfall as the rest of South Florida, but water drains quickly through the sandy soil. As a result, the land is never covered with water. In these dry places, lightning strikes sometimes start wildfires that destroy all but the most fire-resistant plants.

Pinelands are not limited to Big Cypress Swamp. A large pineland area called Long Pine Key thrives in the heart of Everglades National Park. Throughout Everglades pinelands, scrawny slash pines rise into the sky, while a thick undergrowth of spiky-leaved saw palmettos carpets the ground. The roots of both slash pines and saw palmettos spread out over a wide area and extend deep into tiny crevices in the underlying bedrock. Scattered among the pines, several dozen species of tropical hardwoods stretch skyward.

During the day, pinelands are filled with the drumming of woodpeckers and the songs of finches, vireos, and warblers. Far below the treetops, scorpions, centipedes, and millipedes hunt insects. Every so often, a chipmunk darts out of its hiding place and collects some of the seeds that litter the ground. Meanwhile, small flocks of quail and turkeys survey the area for tender green plants.

**VIREO *(VIREO)***

# THE FLORIDA WILD TURKEY
## (Meleagris gallopavo osceola)

Most of the turkeys eaten on Thanksgiving are raised on farms, but wild turkeys are common in many parts of North America. Scientists estimate that as many as one hundred thousand Florida wild turkeys live in Everglades pinelands, hammocks, and cypress swamps.

Although the Florida wild turkey is smaller, slimmer, and darker than other wild turkeys, its lifestyle is very similar. In the spring, male turkeys, called toms, spend quite a bit of time trying to attract the attention of females, called hens. The toms gobble loudly, spread their fan-shaped tails, and strut around. After the turkeys pair up and mate, each hen searches for a secret nesting site and scratches out a shallow hollow. Over the next two weeks, she lays a dozen eggs. The hen protects her growing clutch by covering the eggs with leaves.

When the hen has laid her last egg, she settles down on her clutch and keeps the eggs safe and warm for nearly one month. As soon as she hears the young moving inside their eggs, she inspects the eggs and clucks softly. Her wait is almost over.

Using an egg tooth on the tip of its beak, each poult, or young turkey, pecks a large hole in the end of its egg. Over the next few hours, the damp chicks emerge from their eggs. Less than twenty-four hours later, the mother turkey leads her poults out of the nest and into the world. In this short time, the youngsters have learned to recognize their mother and respond to her clucking calls as well as to her warning cries.

As the turkey family wanders through the pineland or swamp, the birds frequently stop and peck at the ground for seeds and insects. By the time the poults are three weeks old, they can fly short distances. By late fall, the turkeys are full grown. They spend their days foraging. At night, they roost in trees, where they are safe from predators.

As the sun's last rays sink below the horizon, pineland butterflies stop feeding on flower nectar and find a safe place to rest until morning. Not long after they vanish, a different army of winged wonders appears. As the moon's soft glow illuminates the sky, moths flit about the pineland in search of food and mates.

Below them, a female bobcat silently creeps through the dense undergrowth in search of prey. She spots a mouse and grabs it by the neck. But she doesn't kill the rodent. She zigzags through the pineland until she reaches her warm, safe den in a thick clump of saw palmetto. Then she drops the mouse by her three purring kittens.

When the babies were born a few weeks ago, they could not see or hear. Feeding on nothing but their mother's milk, the kittens grew quickly. Now they are ready to start eating meat. After the kittens play with the mouse for a while, their mother shows them how to kill it. Then she lets them devour the prey.

Meanwhile, three black bear cubs are growing up too. When they were born, the cubs weighed less than 1 pound (0.5 kilogram). They were blind and had very little hair. They spent most of their time in a den surrounded by thick saw palmettos. Between naps, they fed greedily on their mother's milk.

Now the bear cubs are old enough to scramble along behind their mother as she searches for food. She shows them the best places to find acorns, palmetto berries, and cabbage palm seeds. If these foods are in short supply, the bears dine on insects, young birds, or small mammals. After a long day of foraging, each cub climbs a different tree and sleeps soundly until morning. Their mother sleeps nearby in a secluded spot on the ground.

As the bear family searches for breakfast, a male bald eagle lifts off from its large stick nest high atop a slash pine. While the male's lifelong mate incubates the couple's single egg, he hunts for both of them. He spends a few minutes surveying the pineland forest floor for snakes and small mammals, then moves on. To find the prey he is really after, the eagle must travel to another part of the Everglades region.

# CHAPTER 4

# A LANDSCAPE SHAPED BY SALT

The bald eagle rises higher and higher into the bright blue sky. Using his long, wide wings to catch breezes of warm air rising from the earth's surface, the bird soars through the sky without much effort. Cruising along at 40 miles (over 60 kilometers) per hour, it takes the eagle just a few minutes to reach the narrow band of mangrove forest that fringes the southwestern coast of Florida.

First he passes over areas where bushy white mangroves grow scattered among other kinds of plants. As the eagle nears Florida Bay, the mangroves become more and more dominant. Most Everglades plants cannot tolerate the high level of salt in the soil, but white mangroves can. Although these trees absorb salt when seawater washes inland twice a day at high tide, they have a way to get rid of the excess salt.

**WHITE MANGROVES (LAGUNCULARIA RACEMOSA)**

Two small glands on each petiole—the small stem that attaches a leaf to a branch—excrete, or discharge, the salt.

The salt in ocean water is very similar to the salt you sprinkle on your french fries. It consists mostly of sodium chloride. Seawater may also contain small amounts of more than fifty other kinds of salts. Scientists determine how salty water is by measuring its salinity, or saltiness, in parts per thousand (ppt)—the number of grams of dissolved salts in 1,000 grams of water. The salinity of freshwater is usually less than 0.5 ppt, while ocean water averages 30 to 35 ppt. The water in South Florida's mangrove forests falls somewhere in between.

Although white mangroves can endure more salt than most other plants, they have their limit. But black mangroves have an additional adaptation that allows them to live in even saltier water. They can excrete salt through dozens of pores on the underside of their leaves. The bottoms of black mangrove leaves are often heavily coated with salt crystals.

It's easy to tell the difference between black mangroves and white mangroves. The roots of black mangroves send up 12-inch-long (30-centimeter-long), fingerlike extensions called pneumatophores. Like the knees of cypresses, pneumatophores probably help black mangroves absorb carbon dioxide from the air and release oxygen. While plants do not breathe the same way humans do, they need this exchange of gases to fuel photosynthesis and to keep nutrients flowing through them.

Further increases in salinity cause black mangroves to give way to a third

> THE SALT IN OCEAN WATER IS VERY SIMILAR TO THE SALT YOU SPRINKLE ON YOUR FRENCH FRIES. IT CONSISTS MOSTLY OF SODIUM CHLORIDE. SEAWATER MAY ALSO CONTAIN SMALL AMOUNTS OF MORE THAN FIFTY OTHER KINDS OF SALTS.

type of mangrove tree. The red mangrove can tolerate even more salt than its relatives. This low, bushy tree has thin prop roots that arch outward from the trunk and some of the larger branches. Small breathing pores along the roots allow the tree to exchange gases with the air. The prop roots also help support the tree, especially during treacherous tropical storms. Most important, a red mangrove's special roots help it repel salt, so that salt never enters the tree's tissues.

The red mangrove has an unusual way of producing and scattering seedlings.

Most flowering plants produce seeds inside a fruit, which either falls to the ground or is eaten by an animal. When the fruit falls to the ground, it rots and releases its seeds. When an animal eats a fruit, the seeds pass through the creature's digestive system and are deposited in a new location. In both cases, the seeds come in contact with soil. Then they sprout and grow into seedlings.

The seedlings of red mangroves grow directly out of the fruits—while the fruits are still attached to the tree. When the seedlings finally drop off the tree in late summer, they

(ABOVE) **PROP ROOTS OF A RED MANGROVE**
**(RHIZOPHORA MANGLE)**

(RIGHT) **RED MANGROVE SEEDLING**

float to a new location and quickly take root. Within a year, each sapling has developed its own tangle of prop roots. For the rest of its life, the hardy evergreen will spread outward in every direction. It loses a few of its shiny, dark green leaves at a time, but never sheds them all at once.

## A LIFE FOR THE BIRDS

As the bald eagle flies above the dense thicket of red mangroves, he scans the water's wavy surface with his sharp eyes. Spotting the telltale flash of a fish's scales, the bird dives steeply.

Why does an eagle look for a flash of scales? Most fish are dark on the top and sides, but have a light-colored belly. This countershading is the perfect camouflage for water creatures. When a predator looks up from below, the fish's light underside blends with sunlight streaming down from above. And when a hungry eagle, brown pelican, or osprey looks down from above, the fish's upper body blends in with the dark water around it. Only the flash of scales in the sun gives the fish away.

As the eagle plummets downward, he never loses sight of his target. It is a tarpon,

**A YOUNG RED MANGROVE HAS TAKEN ROOT NEAR ITS PARENT PLANT.**

a large, acrobatic fish with a dark blue back and a silvery belly. When the master predator reaches the water's surface, he has no trouble snatching the prey with his curved, razor-sharp talons. But the tarpon is so heavy that the eagle cannot lift it out of the water. He must swim to shore by rowing his wings.

When the eagle reaches land, he uses his hooked beak and strong jaws to tear and devour the fish. After eating, the bird catches a smaller fish and carries it back to his hungry mate.

Eagles are not the only birds that hunt in the salty waters that trickle through mangrove forests. Many wading birds spend the summer on the coast after nesting in a cypress swamp during the winter dry season. White ibis use their bills to probe the mud for marine snails, crayfish, crabs, and shrimp. The mangrove swamp also serves as feeding grounds for great white herons, great blue herons, little blue herons, green herons, black-crowned night herons, yellow-crowned night herons, great egrets, snowy egrets, cattle egrets, reddish egrets, roseate spoonbills, and brown pelicans.

(ABOVE) **BROWN PELICAN**
(*PELECANUS OCCIDENTALIS*)

(ABOVE LEFT) **BALD EAGLE**
(*HALIAEETUS LEUCOCEPHALUS*)

(BELOW LEFT) **GREAT EGRET**
(*ARDEA ALBA*)

While herons, egrets, and roseate spoonbills wade through the water, small groups of brown pelicans fly low over the water. They fly in single file, flapping and gliding in unison. When one bird spots a potential meal, it dives headfirst into the water. With a noisy splash, the pelican plunges below the waves. Using its long bill with an expandable pouch, the bird scoops up the fish and returns to the surface. Then the pelican tilts its bill so water can drain out of the pouch and tosses its head back to swallow the food.

Brown pelicans are social birds that do just about everything in groups. In March or April, the birds pair up and mate. Then each couple searches for a suitable nesting site. Working as a team, they build a nest in the middle of a crowded colony. Then the female lays two to four chalky white eggs.

By the end of May, the colony is full of blind, featherless hatchlings. They are completely dependent on their parents. Like all young birds, pelican chicks face many dangers. Unable to fly, they are easy targets for hungry raccoons that sneak into the nests while the young birds sleep.

After eating a chick or two, a raccoon may shimmy down the tree and probe the water's edge for shellfish.

It takes just a few minutes for the predator to crack open and suck down six coon oysters. Alerted to the danger, a female fiddler crab scurries out of harm's way. Safe inside a neighbor's burrow, the little animal settles down to rest until morning.

## REPTILE ROUNDUP

Green sea turtles are not the only turtles that spend time in the mangrove swamps of South Florida. From May to September, several species migrate from their deep-ocean foraging grounds to the Everglades region to breed. These turtles include Atlantic hawksbills, Atlantic ridleys, Atlantic loggerheads, and Atlantic leatherbacks.

During nesting season, large groups of sea turtles congregate near the coast. At night, females lumber up the beach until they pass the high-water mark. Using their front flippers, the turtles sweep away sand to create a hollow. Then they lie in the hollow and use their hind flippers to dig a much deeper hole. After about two hours of hard work, each female lays more than one hundred golf ball–sized eggs. The females then return to their watery home. During a two-week period, each female sea turtle lays several clutches on the same beach.

About two months later, the eggs hatch. The tiny turtles scamper out of the hole and down the beach, then dive into the water. Sharks and killer whales are an adult sea turtle's only enemies, but the hatchlings are much more vulnerable. They make an easy meal for raccoons, otters, gulls, wading birds, and large fishes. The little turtles also may be eaten by other reptiles, including young alligators and crocodiles.

South Florida is the only place in the world where alligators and crocodiles live side by side. Alligators can be found in a variety of habitats, including sloughs, sawgrass flatlands, and cypress swamps. Crocodiles, however, inhabit only mangrove swamps. Since alligators can survive in a wider range of habitats, they are much more abundant than crocodiles. Scientists estimate that more than one million alligators inhabit the Everglades region, but there are fewer than two thousand crocodiles.

## DECOMPOSERS AT WORK

Fiddler crabs (*above*) are only about 1 inch (3 centimeters) long, but they play an important role in the Everglades ecosystem. These feisty, ten-legged shellfish are decomposers that feed on detritus—tiny bits of decomposing matter and waste products.

As red mangroves grow, their leaves wither and die a few at a time. When a dead leaf drops into the water, it is immediately attacked by microscopic bacteria and fungi. These tiny life-forms break down the leaf and absorb some of the nutrients trapped inside it. As the microorganisms go about their business, the leaf is torn to shreds. Eventually, nothing is left but tiny particles of detritus.

These small bits of decaying matter drift with the tide and become an important source of food for a variety of invertebrates and small fishes. When the tide goes out, a fiddler crab scrambles out of its underground burrow and feasts on the detritus. Using its claws, the crab scoops clumps of mud into its mouth. Then the little animal uses its specialized mouthparts to sift through the mud and find the tasty morsels. When the crab has finished its meal, it spits out the leftover mud.

Alligators and crocodiles look similar, but you can tell them apart by looking at their heads. An alligator has a broad, rounded snout, while a crocodile's snout is longer and more pointed. A crocodile's body tends to be longer and skinnier than an alligator's. Most adult American alligators are 6 to 12 feet (2 to 4 meters) long, but an adult American crocodile may be more than 15 feet (4.6 meters) long.

In late May, after mating, female crocodiles leave the mangrove swamp and swim to one of the keys, or small islands, in Florida Bay. Each crocodile searches the sandy shoreline until she finds the perfect spot to lay her eggs. After digging a shallow hole, the mother deposits her clutch and covers the nest with sand and mud. This helps keep the eggs warm while the young are developing.

For the next few months, the female guards the nest day and night. When the hatchlings crack open their eggs, they make croaking noises to alert their mother. She uncovers the tiny crocs, gently picks them up in her mouth, and raises them to ground level. If any youngsters fail to hatch, she gently cracks the eggshells in

her mouth so the little crocs can escape.

The hatchlings head straight for the water, where they will be safer from predators. But some are not fast enough to escape a sharp-eyed black skimmer. The large bird dives down and snatches a wriggling hatchling in his bill, flips the croc into the air, and swallows it. After grabbing a second croc, he lets out a series of loud, shrill squawks, inviting all his skimmer friends to the feast.

In just minutes, more than a dozen black skimmers arrive, but they dare not go after the hatchlings. The bird's call has also alerted the mother crocodile. The birds don't stand a chance against the adult reptile, so they rise higher into the sky and soar away. Perhaps they will have better luck hunting somewhere else.

## HURRICANES LEAVE THEIR MARK

While the other skimmers cruise above the water in search of fish, the successful hunter flies to a sandy flatland along the coast. Back at his nest, he feeds the prey to his hungry chicks. While the little birds eat, both parents stay alert. They know that gulls or little terns may try to steal the catch. After all, they have their own chicks to feed.

Skimmers are closely related to gulls and terns, and the birds often nest together among dense mats of pickerelweed, glasswort, sea purlane, and saltwort. These hardy, salt-tolerant plants grow in places where hurricanes have recently crashed onto the coast and uprooted all the mangrove trees.

After a few weeks, the young skimmers begin to explore their world.

(ABOVE) **A BABY AMERICAN CROCODILE (CROCODYLUS ACUTUS) EMERGES FROM ITS EGGSHELL.**

(LEFT) **AMERICAN CROCODILE**

There is plenty for the little birds to see. Near one edge of the crowded colony, a tern has spotted a raccoon stealing eggs from a nest. The tern lets out a shrill cry of alarm that alerts the entire community. A group of birds dives at the raccoon to chase it away.

In another area of the colony, a male laughing gull is searching for a mate. When he meets a female, both birds stretch their bodies upright, face one another, turn away, and then face each other again. A few minutes later, the male regurgitates some food and offers it to the female. Has this impressed her enough to mate with him?

The little skimmers will never know. They are distracted by two shadows streaking across the sand. Overhead, a small hawk called a harrier chases a seaside sparrow.

As dusk falls over the coastal flatland, the little skimmers return to their nest. Soon all the adult birds return too, and the entire colony of birds settles down for the night. Across the Everglades region, other animals are also preparing to sleep. Wading birds fly to their roosting spots. Otters return to their dens, and marsh rabbits scramble into their burrows.

But not all Everglades creatures are ready for bed. As the sun sinks below the horizon, another group of animals begins to stir. Owls and alligators, moths and mosquitoes, bats and bobcats all emerge. And when a new day dawns, the Everglades ecosystem's never-ending cycles of sleeping and waking, eating and being eaten, giving birth and dying will continue as they have for thousands of years.

BLACK SKIMMERS (*RYNCHOPS NIGER*)

# CHAPTER 5

# MAINTAINING THE BALANCE

The Everglades region is a complex and dynamic ecosystem that includes half a dozen different plant communities and a diverse assortment of animals, fungi, protists, and bacteria. The interactions between these organisms and their physical environment create the ecosystem. They also guarantee its long-term health.

As long as producers, consumers, and decomposers all do their jobs, energy and nutrients will continue to cycle through the environment. And as long as physical conditions remain more or less the same, organisms will have the adaptations they need to do their jobs.

> THE EVERGLADES REGION IS A COMPLEX AND DYNAMIC ECOSYSTEM THAT INCLUDES HALF A DOZEN DIFFERENT PLANT COMMUNITIES AND A DIVERSE ASSORTMENT OF ANIMALS, FUNGI, PROTISTS, AND BACTERIA.

In this way, the living and nonliving components of the ecosystem work together to maintain an overall state of equilibrium, or balance.

A healthy ecosystem can respond to changes and eventually rebalance itself. How well an ecosystem is able to recover depends on its biodiversity—how many different species it supports. The more diverse an ecosystem is, the better it is at weathering change. For thousands of years, the Everglades ecosystem was home to large, healthy populations of many different species. As a result, it was able to survive the stresses of ever-changing water levels and periodic wildfires and hurricanes.

# DEALING WITH DROUGHT

For Everglades organisms, the natural cycle of flood and drought presents both challenges and opportunities. During the wet season, birds, mammals, reptiles, amphibians, fish, and invertebrates spread out over a wide area of land. Food is plentiful, and life is easy. But as drought envelops the region, competition for food intensifies. During this time, each species is put to the test.

Many adult fish die, but the eggs they leave behind survive until the next rainfall. Turtles, frogs, snails, and young alligators burrow deep into the moist mud and rest until conditions improve. Some fish have also developed ways to survive in the mud. Instead of breathing through gills, bowfins absorb oxygen through their skin or use a gas-filled sac called a swim bladder as a makeshift lung. Some small organisms survive by swimming down through crayfish burrows to reach Biscayne Aquifer. This layer of water-bearing rock underlies much of the Everglades region. When rain replenishes the aquifer, the organisms return to the surface.

Many other creatures make their way to the central sloughs. As these watery oases evaporate, catfish, garfish, and tarpon increase their oxygen intake by gulping air at the surface. Killifish, flagfish, golden topminnows, spotfins, sailfin mollies, and mosquito fish have another way of getting oxygen. These fish swim at the surface of the water. Their flat heads and tilted mouths allow them to take in oxygen from the water's thin surface film, which is in direct contact with the air.

Eventually, even the sloughs may dry up. Then there's just one place where aquatic creatures can seek refuge—gator holes. A gator hole is a small pond that an alligator creates in a place where the underlying limestone has weakened and collapsed, forming a natural hollow. The alligator begins its excavation project by slashing the sawgrass with its massive tail and tearing the plants out of the ground with its mighty jaws. Then it drags the vegetation out of the way and uses its hind feet to make the hollow wider and deeper.

Next the alligator piles the dug-up soil around the edges of the pond. This makes the banks higher than the surrounding land. Then the animal architect tunnels into the bank to make a small den for itself. Over the next few months, seeds that land on the banks sprout and grow. Eventually, the pond is surrounded by shrubs and small trees, including pond willows, pond apples, sweet bays, and wax myrtles. These trees are excellent places for insects to feed and for birds to roost year-round.

Because the bottom of a gator hole is lower than the surrounding land, water flows in during the wet season and evaporates very slowly during the dry season. As other parts of the Everglades dry up, fish, frogs, turtles, water snakes, and other aquatic creatures congregate in these small scattered pools. They are soon followed by wading birds in search of an easy meal. Because gator holes provide wading birds with such an abundant and reliable food supply, many have adapted their breeding behavior so they can raise young during the driest part of the year.

A RED MANGROVE (RHIZOPHORA MANGLE) APPEARS STRANDED IN THE DRY SOIL OF THE EVERGLADES' DRY SEASON.

# EVERGLADES ARCHITECTS: ALLIGATORS *(Alligator)*

Alligators are important Everglades inhabitants. Besides building the small, scattered ponds where many other creatures spend the annual "dry-downs," alligators are top predators. As such, they help keep prey populations in check.

During the day, alligators bask in the sun. Like amphibians, fish, and invertebrates, alligators and other reptiles are cold-blooded. This means that an alligator's body temperature matches the temperature of its surroundings. By lying in the sun to warm up, an alligator can make its heart, lungs, brain, and digestive system work more efficiently.

At dusk alligators begin to hunt. They float silently in the water with just their eyes, ears, and nostrils sticking above the water's surface. This allows them to see, hear, and smell approaching prey without being spotted.

The instant a potential meal comes within striking distance, an alligator lunges forward and grabs hold with its sharp, spiky teeth. When it catches small prey, such as fish, water rats, snakes, snails, crabs, or turtles, the alligator points its head up and swallows the meal whole. For larger prey, such as deer, raccoons, otters, or wading birds, the alligator shakes the animal back and forth to break off pieces of flesh that are small enough to swallow.

In midsummer, female alligators dig nests in the soft mud. Then they lay as many as eighty round, leathery eggs and cover the hole. About nine weeks later, the eggs begin to hatch. Young alligators have many enemies, including raccoons, bobcats, otters, owls, snakes, snapping turtles, and wading birds. As a result, very few hatchlings survive their first year. However, once an alligator is about 4 feet (over 1 meter) long, its predators become its prey.

Alligators continue to grow for as long as they live. When alligators are 6 feet (2 meters) in length and about ten years old, they are ready to start families of their own. Some alligators may live to be more than seventy-five years old. These old-timers may be up to 12 feet (4 meters) long.

This survival strategy also benefits the aquatic species. Wading birds remove fish and other prey from gator holes at about the same rate that oxygen is depleted from the water. By gorging themselves, the birds give the remaining creatures a better chance of staying alive until rain renews the land. Then the hardy survivors can spread out and repopulate the rest of the Everglades region.

## WILDFIRES BRING NEW LIFE

In just minutes, a fiery blaze can destroy your home and all your possessions. As a result, people fear fires and do whatever they can to prevent them. When a fire does break out, trained professionals extinguish the flames as quickly as possible. With an attitude like this, it's difficult for most people to understand that wildfires are a natural part of most ecosystems' life cycles.

In the Everglades region, wildfires play an important role in maintaining pinelands. Slash pines and saw palmettos are the main trees in pinelands. But the understory—the trees and shrubs between the tallest-growing trees and the ground cover—often contains many species of tropical hardwoods. These trees grow more quickly than slash pines and have wider canopies. Over time they begin to shade out the pine seedlings, but they usually don't take over completely.

During the summer wet season, towering cumulonimbus clouds form over the Everglades region almost every day. In the late afternoon, these storm clouds shower the land with much-needed water. They also bring crashing thunder and zigzagging streaks of lightning that momentarily brighten the sky. Most of the time, the lightning causes no harm. But if a bolt strikes the bone-dry pine needles that litter a pineland floor, the area may suddenly burst into flames. With no adaptations to tolerate fire, the hardwood understory quickly burns to a crisp. When the smoke finally clears hours or days later, only pines and palmettos are left standing.

How do slash pines and saw palmettos endure fiery blazes? Slash pines have thick, many-layered bark that rarely burns all the way through. The leaves and stems of saw palmettos are destroyed by fire, but the roots extend deep underground. They usually do not burn completely, so they can quickly regenerate the rest of the plant.

When a pineland catches fire, the animals living there must quickly evacuate to wetter areas of the Everglades region. But they aren't displaced for long. As soon as the flames die out, woodpeckers can return to their tapping. Many of the grubs that the woodpeckers eat stayed safe inside their slash pine homes. Within a few days, songbirds return and begin rebuilding their nests.

In just a few weeks, a variety of weedy plants begin to poke up among the charred debris. They grow quickly in the bright sunlight. Soon the burnt land explodes with the bright colors of blossoming wildflowers. Each afternoon a parade of butterflies, including viceroys, hairstreaks, swallowtails, blues, and sulphurs, flutter among the flowers.

One of these butterflies, a female zebra swallowtail, lands on a pink salvia flower. She unfurls her coiled, tonguelike snout, reaches deep inside the flower, and takes a good long sip of sugary nectar. Then the large black-and-yellow butterfly moves on to another plant. As she flits from flower to flower, tiny pollen particles from the flowers stick to the insect's body.

When she lands on another salvia flower, some of the pollen she is carrying falls into the blossom. The pollen grains carry the male sex cells that the flower needs to reproduce. Inside the flower, a sperm cell fuses with an egg cell, and a new plant begins to develop inside a tiny seed.

Unaware of her important role in pollination, the zebra swallowtail continues to feed. When she has finally had her fill, she searches for a passionflower plant. Along its leaves and stem, she lays hundreds of tiny eggs. Passionflower is the only plant that zebra swallowtail caterpillars can eat.

Not all of the butterfly's eggs will hatch, and most of the little caterpillars that emerge will be devoured by hungry birds, spiders, or wasps. Only a small number will survive to become chrysalises. Even fewer will complete metamorphosis and become winged adults.

## A WIND-SHAPED LANDSCAPE

In South Florida's subtropical climate, the entire year's worth of rain falls in just a few months. Summer thunderstorms form offshore as each day heats up. In the late afternoon, they unleash their fury over the land, delivering huge quantities of water.

During the wet season, storms also form farther offshore every day. Occasionally, several of these storms merge and gain additional energy from the warm Caribbean waters. If conditions are right, a low-pressure area develops in the middle of the moving air. As more and more air is pulled into the storm, it begins to spin around the low pressure center. When the storm's winds reach a speed of 74 miles (120 kilometers) per hour, it officially becomes a hurricane.

(ABOVE) **NEW GROWTH APPEARS SHORTLY AFTER FIRES HAVE DIED DOWN.**

(ABOVE RIGHT) **ZEBRA SWALLOWTAIL BUTTERFLY (EURYTIDES MARCELLUS)**

(OPPOSITE PAGE) **WILDFIRES ARE A NATURAL PART OF LIFE IN THE EVERGLADES.**

When a hurricane hits the Florida peninsula, it immediately begins to lose momentum. Most of the time, the hurricane fizzles out in less than twelve hours. But before that happens, torrential rains, powerful winds, and huge waves pummel everything in their path. Large areas of dense mangrove forest are transformed into a sandy wasteland.

Like a pineland devastated by wildfire, the hurricane-ravaged coast begins to rebound almost immediately. Hardy, salt-tolerant plants sprout among the scattered debris. For many years, the landscape is dominated by nesting colonies of shorebirds. Here and there, a lone buttonwood tree rises above the rest of the vegetation. Eventually, mangrove seedlings arrive on the tides and repopulate the land.

## AN ENDANGERED ECOSYSTEM

For thousands of years, the Everglades ecosystem has endured a host of natural disturbances. Through floods and droughts, wildfires and hurricanes, the land and the life-forms have found ways to rebound. Each time part of the system was knocked out of whack, other areas compensated until balance was restored.

But every ecosystem has its limits. If physical conditions change too much or if entire populations of organisms are killed off, the effects may be felt throughout the entire ecosystem. It is hard to imagine a single force powerful enough to upset the Everglades ecosystem, but such a force does exist. During the twentieth century, humans came very close to destroying one of the most special places in the world.

A GREAT BLUE HERON (ARDEA HERODIAS) PERCHES ON A SNAPPED HARDWOOD PINE, ONE OF MANY LEFT IN THE EVERGLADES IN THE WAKE OF A HURRICANE.

# CHAPTER 6

# HOW PEOPLE AFFECT THE EVERGLADES ECOSYSTEM

On April 12, 1513, the Spanish explorer and conquistador (conqueror) Juan Ponce de León and his crew anchored their ship just north of the present-day city of St. Augustine. The sailors claimed the land for Spain, giving it the name Florida. Then they followed the coastline southward, rounded the tip of the peninsula, and continued north into the Gulf of Mexico before returning to Puerto Rico.

Although Ponce de León spent many hours exploring the mangrove swamps that wrap Florida's southern and western coasts, he never reached the interior of the Everglades region. For the next two hundred years, a Native American group called the Calusas were the only humans who visited the sawgrass marshlands and cypress swamps.

The Calusas lived in harmony with nature. But when colonial settlers arrived in Florida in the 1700s and 1800s, they did not treat the land or its inhabitants with the same kind of respect. They thought of the Everglades region as a worthless wetland where mosquitoes buzzed and snakes bred. The Europeans dreamed of draining the entire area and developing it into something "useful." For thousands of years, the Calusas had blended seamlessly into the Everglades ecosystem. In less than 150 years, the newcomers from Europe completely altered it.

## THE BATTLE AGAINST NATURE BEGINS

Shortly after Florida joined the United States in 1845, Congress passed a law allowing 20 million acres (8 million hectares) of the new state to be drained and logged. Following the Civil War

(1861–1865), ambitious land developers began tampering with nature—and they haven't stopped since. The Caloosahatchee River was extended all the way to Lake Okeechobee so that excess lake water could be transported to the Gulf of Mexico. Developers built a water-retaining levee along Lake Okeechobee's southern rim. A series of canals funneled water from the lake to the Atlantic Ocean.

In the 1940s, the U.S. Army Corps of Engineers got involved in this massive replumbing effort. Congress had authorized the corps to do whatever was necessary to control Everglades flooding and supply freshwater to the state's growing human population. By 1960 more than 1,400 miles (2,200 kilometers) of drainage canals crisscrossed the Everglades region. A dike contained the water of Lake Okeechobee, converting it into a giant reservoir. Additional water was held in three large water conservation areas to the east of Big Cypress Swamp.

Although the Everglades ecosystem desperately needed that water, natural areas had last dibs. The government had other priorities. The land to the south of Lake Okeechobee was transformed from wetland to farmland. Known as the Everglades Agricultural Area, this area covers 700,000 acres (300,000 hectares) and is used to grow sugarcane and winter vegetables. Water for these crops is channeled from the lake and the water conservation areas through a vast network of irrigation pipes.

An even larger share of the precious water goes to the seaside cities that began to spring up in the early part

**FOLLOWING THE CIVIL WAR, AMBITIOUS LAND DEVELOPERS BEGAN TAMPERING WITH NATURE—AND THEY HAVEN'T STOPPED SINCE.**

of the twentieth century. After loggers felled the pinelands growing on top of the Atlantic Coastal Ridge, land developers quickly began constructing vacation resorts and permanent housing. Following World War I (1914–1918), seasonal tourists and year-round residents poured into Fort Lauderdale, Miami, and Fort Myers.

As the area's population grew, so did its water requirements. A system of canals diverted water from the Everglades to the coastal communities. To ensure good ocean views, city planners ordered that the mangroves growing along the shoreline be removed and replaced by palm trees. Little by little, the Everglades ecosystem was being degraded or destroyed. Would anyone stand up and take notice?

## A CHANGE IN THINKING

In 1968 a team of bulldozers rolled across the southeast corner of Big Cypress Swamp, uprooting everything in their path. This was the start of yet another major project—the largest international airport in the world. According to plans, the ultramodern facility would claim 39 square miles (100 square kilometers) of swamp.

HOUSING DEVELOPMENTS LIKE THIS ONE BEGAN TO SPRING UP IN THE EVERGLADES REGION DURING THE DECADES FOLLOWING WORLD WAR I.

But the loss of land would be only a minor part of the airport's overall impact on the environment. It would generate a huge amount of sewage and jet engine pollutants. Scientists and concerned citizens across the country began to question the merit of the project. Facing a deluge of protests, planners were forced to halt work on the airport. Finally government officials shut down the project permanently.

This decision was a tremendous victory for the Everglades ecosystem and a turning point for the United States. In the past, few people had looked beyond the human benefits of a development project to examine the long-term impact on the environment. But attitudes were changing.

People were beginning to understand the value of natural areas. Wetlands prevent or reduce flooding and erosion, and they provide drinking water. Wetlands also remove large quantities of carbon dioxide—one of the greenhouse gases responsible for global warming—from the air.

Many wetlands purify contaminated water. As water moves through a wetland, plants trap pollutants in their tissues, removing them from the environment.

THE PLANT LIFE IN THE EVERGLADES HELPS TO PURIFY THE WATER THAT PASSES THROUGH THE ECOSYSTEM. WATER LILIES *(NYMPHAEACEAE)* (ABOVE) AND RED MANGROVES *(RHIZOPHORA MANGLE)* (RIGHT) ARE JUST SOME OF THE PLANTS THAT CONTRIBUTE TO THIS PROCESS.

Wetland bacteria break down a variety of dangerous chemicals into harmless compounds. Water leaving a wetland is often much cleaner than when it entered.

During the 1970s, Congress passed the Federal Water Pollution Act, the Endangered Species Act, and other important environmental legislation. The new laws provided funding for scientists to assess the damage and propose solutions. Researchers working in Florida made a startling discovery. Although large areas of the Everglades region still looked like the traditional ecosystem, they were not functioning like they were supposed to. Even Everglades National Park was in danger—and still is.

## THE DAMAGE WE'VE DONE

Rerouting Everglades water has disrupted the region's seasonal cycles of flood and drought. Because so much water is diverted to cities and farms, many natural areas receive too little water. In these places, plants, fish, and amphibians are dying. Meanwhile insect populations are increasing because they have fewer predators.

Other parts of the Everglades ecosystem get plenty of water, but at the wrong times. Year after year, the nests of alligators and seaside sparrows flood. Apple snail eggs are drowned. Wading birds have trouble raising families because fish are not forced to congregate in sloughs and gator holes.

As the amount of water flowing through the Everglades ecosystem has decreased, salty water from Florida Bay has begun to back up into low-lying areas. The increased salinity has killed seagrass, leaving fish and invertebrates with nothing to eat. When these creatures die, so do their predators. Saltwater has also made its way into the underwater aquifers that supply many people with drinking water.

Even when the right amount of water arrives at the right times, Everglades creatures must face yet another challenge. Much of the water pumped into the remaining natural areas of the Everglades ecosystem has passed through the agricultural areas just south of Lake Okeechobee. Along the way, the water picks up nitrogen and phosphorus, two nutrients used to fertilize the fields. Sawgrass-covered flatlands are naturally low in phosphorus. When too much phosphorus is added to the water, phosphorus-loving cattail plants quickly crowd out the natural vegetation. Eventually the organisms that live or feed on sawgrass disappear too.

Cattails are not the only plants that are spreading too quickly in the Everglades ecosystem. During the last century, a variety of exotic, or nonnative, species have been introduced, either accidentally or on purpose. Some of these alien invaders threaten the food web of the entire biological community.

In 1906 the first melaleuca trees were planted in the Everglades. Native to Australia, these plants grow well in warm, wet climates and are resistant to fire. Developers hoped that the water-loving melaleucas would help drain the wetlands and provide a good source of timber. But the trees spread much more quickly than anyone expected. They have taken over and dried out land once occupied by sloughs and sawgrass.

When developers built grand resort hotels, they often surrounded them with beautiful gardens full of exotic plants. One of their favorite species was the Brazilian pepper, a small tree native to South America. As birds spread the seeds of these hardy plants far beyond the seaside gardens, the trees began to crowd out many native hammock and cypress swamp species. Because Brazilian peppers grow in tight clusters, they don't provide nesting places for wading birds.

Plants are not the only invaders causing trouble for the Everglades region's native

**CATTAILS (TYPHA)**

inhabitants. Cuban tree frogs gobble up smaller native species, while a fish called the blue tilapia devours huge quantities of aquatic plants that normally provide cover for smaller Everglades fishes. The Asian swamp eel is a hardy, air-breathing fish that sucks up the foods wading birds need to survive. Scientists estimate that the number of wading birds living in the Everglades region plummeted by 90 percent during the twentieth century.

While Asian swamp eels have contributed to this startling loss, humans have played a far greater role in the decline of wading birds. Tampering with Everglades water levels has proved disastrous for the nesting success of wood storks.

During the late 1800s, thousands of egrets, herons, and spoonbills were killed for their plumes, which were used to adorn ladies' hats. Ruthless hunters often shot the birds as they incubated their eggs, ensuring that a new generation would never hatch.

Luckily, fashions come and go. By the 1940s, plumed hats fell out of favor, and the remaining wading birds stood a fighting chance. Although greatly reduced in number, they continue to hang on.

(ABOVE) **CUBAN TREE FROG**
*(OSTEOPILUS SEPTENTRIONALIS)*

(RIGHT) **BIRDS LIKE THE GREAT EGRET *(ARDEA ALBA)* WERE HUNTED TO NEAR EXTINCTION DURING THE 1800S. THEIR BEAUTIFUL FEATHERS WERE USED TO DECORATE LADIES' HATS.**

## THE FUTURE OF THE EVERGLADES ECOSYSTEM

During the 1990s, both the state of Florida and the U.S. Congress began setting aside money for programs that would help preserve and protect the Everglades region. In 2000 Congress approved a landmark bill to save this unique and precious natural area. Over a forty-year period, the bill will provide $7.8 billion for a series of projects aimed at saving sixty-eight species of threatened and endangered plants and animals. At the same time, the needs of farmers and residents will be addressed. With the guidance of environmental scientists, engineers will undo a century's worth of damage in order to restore the natural flow of water throughout South Florida.

The ambitious plan calls for nearly seventy separate projects. They will restore the natural path of the Kissimmee River, remove nearly 250 miles (400 kilometers) of canals that dump water from Lake Okeechobee into the ocean, and construct reservoirs to hold freshwater until it is needed. But that's just the beginning. More than 100,000 acres (40,000 hectares) of farmland will be converted back into wetland, and pollution from fertilizers will be significantly reduced. In addition, scientists will develop techniques for controlling the spread of exotic species.

If everything goes according to plan, wood storks will eventually have no trouble feeding their chicks, sawgrass will no longer be choked out by cattails, and home owners along the Florida coast will have plenty of water. Although there are still many, many hurdles to overcome, scientists, engineers, government agencies, farmers, business owners, and concerned citizens are confident that by working together they can make the dream come true.

**GREAT EGRET *(ARDEA ALBA)***

# WHAT YOU CAN DO

One of the best ways to learn about the Everglades region is to visit it. Everglades National Park, Big Cypress National Preserve, Corkscrew Swamp Sanctuary, Loxahatchee National Wildlife Refuge, and Collier-Seminole State Park all have nature study programs and interpretive trails that teach people about the wildlife of South Florida. By staying on the trails, you can enjoy your surroundings and know that you are causing no harm.

To protect the Everglades region and other wetlands, citizens must make informed choices about how they use the areas. What can you do to protect wetlands near your home? Here are some suggestions.

• If you fish, be careful not to spread exotic species from one body of water to another. Use separate gear in each body of water. Do not catch small fish in one place and use them as bait in another spot. If you catch an exotic species, release it immediately into the same body of water. Take a shower and wash your clothes as soon as you get home, so no eggs will accidentally enter another waterway.

• Don't pour chemicals such as gasoline, paint, or household cleaners into sinks, bathtubs, or toilets or onto the ground. These chemicals may seep into a groundwater system and pollute it. When the poison comes into contact with fish and other aquatic creatures, it can kill them. Contact a local government agency to find out whether your town or city has a day designated for the safe collection and disposal of chemicals.

• Use safe alternatives to harsh household cleaners. Instead of commercial window cleaner, try a mixture of vinegar and water. A paste of baking soda and water safely and effectively cleans sinks, tubs, and toilets.

• Don't throw trash and other garbage into a roadside ditch or any body of water. Not only is trash ugly, but it can also make fish and other animals sick. Some communities have water cleanup days.

You might want to participate in one. If you do, be sure to go with an adult and remember to wear gloves and boots.

- Conserve water. It may not seem like much, but each time you get a drink and let the faucet run until the water gets cold, you're wasting water. Keep a water bottle in the refrigerator. You should also avoid letting the water run continuously while you're washing your hands and face or brushing your teeth. Take showers rather than baths. A typical bath requires twice as much water as most showers.
- Use wood chips or bricks rather than concrete for pathways, so rain can seep into the ground. Less runoff means that pesticides and fertilizers are less likely to find their way into wetlands and other watery environments.
- Collect rainwater in a barrel and use it to water plants around your house. Keep the barrel tightly covered when it isn't raining to prevent mosquitoes from laying eggs in it.
- Join a community organization that takes an active role in wetland preservation and conservation.

## YOU CAN BE INVOLVED IN FUTURE PLANNING

If you live in South Florida, you can contact local organizations that are involved in preserving the Everglades ecosystem. You can also read local newspapers and magazines to learn more about efforts to restore the Everglades. Or you can write letters to the governor of your state and your state senators and representatives. Your input can really make a difference!

**To write to the senators from your state:**
The Honorable (name of your senator)
United States Senate
Washington, DC 20510

**To write to your representative in Congress:**
The Honorable (name of your representative)
U.S. House of Representatives
Washington, DC 20515

# WEBSITES TO VISIT FOR MORE INFORMATION

### Big Cypress National Preserve

<http://www.nps.gov/bicy/>

You can learn about upcoming events, nearby accommodations, and the history of the preserve.

### The Everglades

<http://www.miamisci.org/ecolinks/everglades/index.html>

Teachers and students from Avocado Elementary School in Homestead, Florida, have studied the Everglades in depth. This site summarizes many of the things they learned about the land and the creatures that live there.

### Everglades Field Trip

<http://www.env.duke.edu/wetland/e_subdiv.htm>

This site, maintained by the Duke University Wetland Center, features excellent, up-to-date descriptions of South Florida's parks and preserves.

### Everglades National Park

<http://www.nps.gov/ever/>

This is the National Park Service's official website. You can find out about Everglades National Park's history and read about the junior ranger program for kids. Links will take you to a page with information about South Florida's natural history.

# FOR FURTHER READING

Blaustein, Daniel. *The Everglades and the Gulf Coast.* Tarrytown, NY: Benchmark Books, 2000.

Douglas, Marjory Stoneman. *The Everglades: River of Grass.* Sarasota, FL: Pineapple Press, 1947.

Lourie, Peter. *Everglades: Buffalo Tiger and the River of Grass.* Honesdale, PA: Boyds Mills Press, 1998.

Lucas, Eileen. *Everglades.* Austin, TX: Raintree/Steck-Vaughn, 1995.

Matthiessen, Peter. *Killing Mister Watson.* New York: Vintage Books, 1991.

Toops, Connie. *The Florida Everglades.* Stillwater, MN: Voyageur Press, 1998.

# GLOSSARY

**alga (pl. algae):** a simple primary producer that often lives in water or on damp surfaces

**bacterium (pl. bacteria):** a single-celled organism that lives in soil, water, air, or the bodies of plants and animals

**biodiversity:** the number of different species living in an area

**biome:** a category of naturally existing communities of living organisms. Forests, deserts, wetlands, and lakes are all biomes.

**cold-blooded:** an animal with a body temperature that matches its environment, rather than remaining constant

**decomposer:** an organism that breaks down plant and animal matter into simple nutrients that can be used again by plants

**detritus:** tiny bits of decomposing material in a body of water

**ecosystem:** a specific community of organisms and their physical environment, which includes climate, soil, water, and air

**exotic species:** an organism that has been transplanted to a new environment

**fungus (pl. fungi):** an organism that does not perform photosynthesis and must absorb nutrients through its cell walls. Fungi include molds, rusts, and yeasts.

**glacier:** a large, moving body of snow and ice

**habitat:** the kind of environment in which a species normally lives

**hammock:** an elevated area of land in the Everglades region where a mixture of tropical and temperate trees grow

**hydroperiod:** the amount of time an area of land is underwater each year

**invertebrate:** an animal that doesn't have a backbone

**marsh:** a wetland that is flooded for most or all of the year. It cannot support trees.

**metamorphosis:** the series of steps by which some young animals, such as insects or frogs, transform into adults

**migrate:** to move from one area to another for feeding or breeding, usually during a particular season

**molt:** to shed or lose the exoskeleton, feathers, skin, or other outer covering

**nymph:** the young of an insect that develops through incomplete metamorphosis

**periphyton:** a mat composed of tiny living things and the mineral calcite

**petiole:** the small stem that attaches a leaf to a branch

**photosynthesis:** the process by which plants and certain other organisms use sunlight, carbon dioxide, and water to make their own food

**pneumatophore:** a long, thin, above-ground structure that is part of a black mangrove tree's root system

**primary consumer:** an organism that eats plants

**primary producer:** an organism that uses photosynthesis to make food

**protist:** a member of the group of simple organisms that are neither plants nor animals

**salinity:** the amount of salt in water, soil, or the air

**secondary consumer:** an animal that eats other animals

**sediment:** small pieces of rock, soil, and plant debris

**slough:** a wetland that contains more water than a marsh or swamp; the bottom is covered with a deep layer of mud

**spinneret:** an organ for producing threads of silk

**swamp:** a wetland that is flooded for at least part of the year and can support trees

**swim bladder:** an air-filled organ that many fish species use to control the depth at which they swim. A few species of fish can also use it to store oxygen.

**warm-blooded:** an animal that maintains a constant body temperature

**water table:** the top of the part of the ground that is soaked with water

**wetland:** an area where the water table lies close to the surface for most of the year

# INDEX

air plants, 25, 29
algae, 22–23
alligators, 19, 23, 32, 44, 46–47, 48, 50–53, 61
apple snails, 22, 23, 61
aquatic plants, 17–18

bears, 37
Big Cypress Swamp, 28–37
biodiversity, 15, 49
birds, 15, 18–19, 24–25, 31, 35, 51, 61, 63; anhinga, 19; bald eagle, 37–38, 41–42; black skimmer, 47–48; brown pelican, 41–43; egrets, 22, 32–33, 42–43, 63; Florida wild turkey, 36; herons, 18–19, 24, 32, 42–43, 56; ibis, 32–33, 42; owls, 27–29, 48, 52; purple gallinule, 18, 19; snail kite, 23–24; storks, 31–33, 63
Biscayne Aquifer, 50
bladderwort, 13, 18
bobcat, 33–34, 37, 48
butterflies, 37, 54; zebra swallowtail, 54–55

Calusa Indians, 57
cattails, 62
Corkscrew Swamp Sanctuary, 31
crocodiles, 44, 46–47
cypresses, 6, 13, 17, 28–29, 30, 31; "knees," 29

deer, 20, 22, 30, 52

drought, 12, 15, 50–51, 56, 61

ecosystems, 6–7
elevation, 12–13, 15
energy, 7, 23, 30, 49, 55
Everglades Agricultural Area, 58
exotic species, 62–63, 64, 66

fiddler crabs, 44, 45
fish, 15, 18–19, 41–42, 48, 50, 61; Asian swamp eel, 63; bowfin, 50; tarpon, 41–42, 50
frogs, 22; Cuban tree, 63; pig, 22

gator holes, 50–51, 53, 61
glaciers, 10–11
grasshoppers, 26–27

hardwood hammocks, 13, 24–25, 27, 35, 62
hurricanes, 15, 47, 55–56

insects, 18, 26, 27
invertebrates, 18, 22, 24, 50

Kissimmee River, 16, 64

mangroves, 6, 15, 38–41, 42, 45–47, 51, 56, 57, 60; black, 39; red, 40–41, 44, 51; white, 38–39
marshes, 6, 13, 16

Native Americans. See Calusa Indians

Okeechobee, Lake, 9, 16–17, 58, 61, 64
otters, 19–20, 23, 44, 48

panther, Florida, 30, 34
people, affects of, 58–64
periphyton, 18
pinelands, 13, 15, 17, 34–35, 37, 53–54, 56, 59
pollution, 60, 61–62, 64
Ponce de León, Juan, 57
preservation, 64, 66–67

raccoons, 20, 23, 25, 30, 32, 43, 44, 48

salt, 15, 38–40, 61
sawgrass, 6, 7, 13, 16–17, 20, 21, 24
Shark River Slough, 17
slash pines, 34–35, 53
sloughs, 6, 13, 15, 16–17, 50, 61
snakes, 25–26; cottonmouth, 30–31
spiders, 27
strangler fig, 25

trees, 24–25, 29, 51; melaleuca, 62; saw palmettos, 35, 37, 53; swamp, 29; tropical, 25, 35, 53. See also cypresses, mangroves
true Everglades, 16–27
turtles, 18, 44, 50

water table, 6
wildfires, 13, 15, 34, 53–54

# ABOUT THE AUTHOR

A careful observer, Melissa Stewart has always been fascinated by the natural world. Before becoming a full-time writer, she earned a bachelor's degree in biology from Union College and a master's degree in science and environmental journalism from New York University. She then spent a decade working as a science editor.

Stewart has written more than a dozen critically acclaimed children's books about animals, ecosystems, earth science, and space science. She has also contributed articles to a variety of magazines for adults and children, including *Science World, ChemMatters, National Geographic World, Odyssey, Wild Outdoor World, Natural New England,* and *American Heritage of Invention and Technology.* She lives in Marlborough, Massachusetts.

# PHOTO ACKNOWLEDGEMENTS

Additional photographs are reproduced with the permission of: © Ben Mangor/SuperStock, p. 9; © Fritz Polking; Frank Lane Picture Agency/CORBIS, p. 20; © Wolfgang Kaehler/CORBIS, p. 22 (top); © Chris Mattison; Frank Lane Picture Agency/CORBIS, p. 22 (bottom); © Gary Meszaros, Photo Researchers, p. 26; © Wayne Bennett/CORBIS , p. 30; © T. Davis, Photo Researchers, p. 34; © Tim Zurowski/CORBIS, p. 35; © Patrick Ward/CORBIS, p. 38; © Jonathan Blair/CORBIS, p. 47; © Nik Wheeler/CORBIS, p. 48; © Ray Coleman, Photo Researchers, p. 55 (right); © Raymond Gehman/CORBIS, p. 56; © Kevin Fleming/CORBIS, p. 59.